# Phonetic Storybook 6

## Short Vowels ă, ĕ, ĭ, ŏ, ŭ

D0033824

PEARSON
Longman

# Contents

## Raceway Step 15
Short Vowel Words

# Pat Has a Spill

By Jean Elsie Cox

Illustrated by Sally Davies

# Vocabulary Words

1. fast
2. fix
3. leg
4. lip
5. mess
6. milk
7. mix
8. neck
9. spill
10. still
11. went

**Story Word**

12. her

Pat gets eggs.

Pat gets ham and milk.

Pat went to mix in the
milk, but the cup fell.
Pat had a spill!

The red mat is wet.
Pat has a big mess.

Pat will get it up fast.
Pat has a rag.

Pat is still a mess.
Pat has milk on her lip,
her neck, and her leg.

Mom will help Pat.
Mom will fix a wet lip.

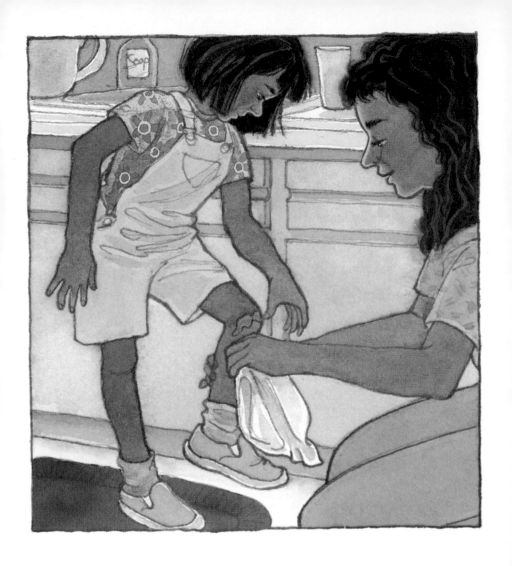

Mom will fix a wet leg
and a wet neck.

Pat is not sad. Pat is
glad. Mom is glad!
**The End**

# The Red Truck

By Sue Dickson

Illustrated by Billy Davis

Step 15 • ă, ĕ, ĭ, ŏ, ŭ

# Vocabulary Words

1. bell
2. block
3. brick
4. bump
5. camp
6. dent
7. drop
8. fills
9. hill
10. lamp
11. lock
12. pest
13. pin
14. runs
15. sled
16. stamp
17. steps
18. stick
19. Ted
20. Ted's
21. vest
22. wig

## Story Words

23. bump-te-bump
24. can not
    cannot

Ted has a truck. The
truck is red. Ted gets gas
in his truck. Ted fills it up.
Ted's red truck runs fast.

The red truck went up a hill. The red truck went past a bell. The red truck went past a well.

The red truck went
past a frog and a log
and a hog.

The red truck went
past a lock and a clock
and a block and a sock.

The red truck went
past a nest and a pest
and a vest.

It went past a lamp and a camp and a stamp.

The red truck went past
a top and a mop. A drop
hit the top of the truck!

It went past a bed and
a sled and ten men and
a hen in a pen!

The red truck went past a pin and a bin and a big, big wig!

It went past a cat
and a mat and a stick
and a brick.

Bump-te-bump-te-bump!
The red truck is bent.
It has a big dent! If Ted
cannot mend it, the big
steps will end it!

**The End**

# West Camp

### By Vida Daly
### Illustrated by Meredith Johnson

# Vocabulary Words

1. back
2. best
3. digs
4. dock
5. flag
6. flaps
7. flip
8. flop
9. grand
10. hands
11. hot
12. jumps
13. kid

14. lumps
15. pond
16. rests
17. Rob
18. sift
19. sits
20. swam
21. swim
22. wind
23. yells

**Story Words**

24. I

in to
25. into

Bill went to camp. The camp is West Camp. West Camp has a flag. It flaps in the wind.

West Camp has a pond.
The pond has a dock. Bill
can jump into the pond
from the dock.

Bill jumps and yells,
"I am a big rock!" Bill
jumps and jumps. It is fun.

His last jump is a
grand jump. Bill ran fast.
It is his best jump.

Bill can kick and swim.
Bill can swim fast and
well. It is fun in
the pond.

Bump! Bump! Bill swam
into Rob, but it was not
a bad bump. Bill and Rob
yell and kick, and flip and
flop. It is a lot of fun!

"I will sit on the sand
to rest," said Bill. Rob sits
and rests with Bill.

Bill digs in the sand
with his hands. The sand
has lumps in it. Bill
cannot sift it well.

"It is hot," said Bill.
"I will jump back into
the pond."

"Last kid in is a wet
hen!" Rob yells.

It is a lot of fun at
West Camp.

**The End**

# The Rust Rug
## (Part 1)

By Sue Dickson

Illustrated by Cheryl Mendenhall

# Vocabulary Words

1. bend

2. fist

3. fuzz

4. hand

5. kids

6. lump

7. pick

8. rust

9. stiff

10. trip

## Story Words

ask

11. asked

12. cost

13. he

Mom went to get a rug. Mom said to the man, "I must get a rug. I will pick a rust rug, not red, but rust."

"I have a rust rug,"
said the man. The man
went to get the rust rug.

"It has the best back,"
said the man. "It will
not bend up and trip
the kids."

"It will not get lumps.
Dust and fuzz will not
stick to it."

The man said, "If the
kids spill milk, it will not
spot the rug."

"Rub a hand on the rug.
It is not stiff," he said.
"Yes, the rust rug is best."

The man hit his fist on the rug. "It is just grand," he said.

"Will the rug cost a lot?" asked Mom.

"It will not cost a lot," said the man.

"I am glad," said Mom.

Mom said, "Dad will get the rug. It will fit in his van."

"Dad will pick it up," said Mom.

"Yes," said the man. "I will help him."

**The End (Part 1)**

# Dad Gets the Rust Rug
## (Part 2)

By Sue Dickson

Illustrated by Cheryl Mendenhall

# Vocabulary Words

1. black

2. desk

3. Meg

4. tack

Dad went to get the
rust rug. Dad went in his
black van.

Dad got the rug from the man. "It is a grand rug," said Dad.

Dad is back. Dad has
the rug. Dad can lift the
rug if Mom, Tim, and
Meg help.

"Pick it up, Tim. Give it a tug, Meg," said Dad.

"At last I have a rust rug!" said Mom.

Dad will tack the rug.
Tap, tap, tap, tap went
Dad. The rug cannot lift
up. It will not bend. It
will not trip the kids.

Dad will set the desk on the rug. Mom will set the lamp on the rug.

"It is a grand rug," said Mom.

"Yes," said Dad, "but the kids must not get milk on it."

"The kids must not get gum on it," said Mom.

"The kids must not get jam on it," said Dad. "Jam will stick to it."

"Meg and Tim, the rug must not get gum and jam on it. Gum and jam will stick to it. The rug must not get a mess on it," said Mom.

"Yes," said Meg. "Tim and I will just rest on the rug. It will be fun. The rust rug is just grand!"

**The End (Part 2)**

# Rick's Band

by Sue Dickson

Illustrated by Laura Jacobsen

# Vocabulary Words

1. band
2. Bob
3. Don
4. drum
5. Gwen
6. Rick
7. strum

**Story Word**

8. Rick's

Don has a drum.
Bob can strum.

Gwen can hum. Rick
will tap.

Rick has a band. "A band is a lot of fun," said Rick.

**The End**

## Sound-Spelling Correspondence:

ă, ĕ, ĭ, ŏ, ŭ

## High Frequency Words:

| | | |
|---|---|---|
| and | is | to |
| have | said | was |
| her | the | with |

## Story Words:

| | | |
|---|---|---|
| asked | he | into |
| cannot | her | |
| cost | I | |

# LONGMAN

## CORNERSTONE
### Phonics and Word Analysis

Phonetic Storybook 6

ă, ě, ĭ, ŏ, ŭ

www.longmancornerstone.com

PEARSON
Longman

ISBN-13: 978-0-13-207500-8
ISBN-10: 0-13-207500-8

EAN

9 780132 075008

90000>

P8-APF-985